When everything is
said and done

I am
infinitely loved

BRIAN GROGAN SJ

First published in 2017 by Messenger Publications

ISBN 978 1 910248 86 7

Designed by Messenger Publications Design Department
Typeset in Baskerville
Printed by Johnswood Press Ltd

Messenger Publications,
37 Lower Leeson Street, Dublin D02 W938
www.messenger.ie

Contents

Welcome!

This is a simple book. On each right hand page you find a verse from Scripture, adjusted to make it personal to yourself. I invite you to take each statement as a divine love note which is trying to convey an important message to you! There is one for each day of the month, and you can find many more for yourself, because God is always trying to get across to you the single great reality that you are endlessly loved! These Scripture love notes are enriching and bring happy surprises. They help you to find the buried treasure which gives meaning to your life no matter what may be its ups and downs. They make you smile more and soften your attitude to people you dislike, since they also are well loved!

On each left hand page is a meditation in the form of a conversation with God which explores an aspect of God's dealings with us. God's ways are often puzzling to us, are contrary to our desires, and so can block our wavering belief that God truly loves us infinitely.

When I shared these scriptural love notes with a friend, he responded, 'These are great, but it's a terrible pity they don't read them in Church!' Of course they do, but they were going over his head: all he needed was to have the door opened a little so he could see that God is always trying to persuade him that he, personally, is limitlessly loved. God is deeply interpersonal: we see Jesus in the gospels engaging with people in a very direct way. 'Come to me!' 'What do you want?' 'Do you love me?' 'Follow me!' So I invite you to 'get personal' and to put your own name in the blank space of each piece of Scripture: then repeat it through the day, until gradually it finds a home in your heart.

I often begin my prayer by allowing God say to me, 'Brian, you are my beloved!' This changes prayer from a boring litany of petitions and distractions to a vibrant encounter, because I am meeting with God directly. I know of nothing better than to keep coming back to such a love notes during my prayer. St Ignatius suggests that just before praying I might ask, 'How does God see me?' So I try to listen to what God is trying to tell me about myself in the love note; this can lead to an experience of wonder and gratitude. Prayer becomes interpersonal, a dialogue between two persons who are in love. This is not strange: after all, our relationship with God is meant to be a love affair! When St Elizabeth of the Trinity was asked what she did in her prayer, she replied, 'Oh, Madam, we spend our time loving one another!' This is what prayer is about. May you come to do the same.

Moses did this! Each day, following instructions he set up the tent of meeting with God outside the Hebrew camp in the desert. A tent suggests closeness, friendship, intimacy and privacy. There he met God face to face, and they chatted as friends about whatever came up. Likewise in the desert of my life, God comes to my little tent of meeting hoping to meet me, and I show up in order to be reminded of how much God loves me. I get directions for the day ahead and to intercede for others. 'I come to you to take your touch before I begin my day.' Moses wouldn't have missed this daily meeting for the world! We are told that his face shone after encountering God, a sign that the meeting enlivened him and made him happy. May your meeting with God be like that!

The cover title for this book comes from Pope Francis and we shall explore its depths. His statement, *'When everything is said and done, we are infinitely loved'* is the single theme of this book, viewed from various angles. The word 'love' is endlessly rich – it comes up 872 times in the Bible, referring then to married and parental love, to the love that sustains friendship and centrally to the love of God for all of us. The word 'infinite' means that God's love for me is endless: no matter how much I stretch it there is always, always more. The images of God that leap out from the Scripture quotations may be richer than those with which you, like me, may have been brought up. This little book offers tasters for a feast: it is for you to further explore this theme with the help of the Spirit of Love. Your exploring need never end!

Do You Simply Love Me?

*D*ear Lord, one of the nicest cards I ever got had only four words on it: 'I simply love you.' At that time this was what I most needed to hear. And, Lord, I always need to hear it from you. I was greatly helped when, a few years ago, Pope Francis wrote in *The Joy of the Gospel* (n.6), 'When everything is said and done, we are infinitely loved'. This massive statement about you, God, means that, no matter how I let you down, you delight in me as I am. I am radically loved; you are totally positive about me. Therapists try – more or less successfully – to develop unconditional positive regard for their clients, else the therapeutic relationship will never take off. This reflects on the human level your regard for each of us. The relationship between you and me can take off only in this atmosphere. So let me believe, no matter what negative stories I carry from childhood, that no-one can love me as you do, that you never turn away from me in despair or boredom and that nothing can increase or diminish your love for me.

Just as the sun heats me without making a choice about it, you don't have to make a choice about loving me: you simply do it! Often I'd prefer that you wouldn't intervene in my life as you do, but if I can believe that your love for me is simple, unconditional, total, like the warmth of the sun, I can manage the rest.

$\mathcal{L}$ord, may I believe that you are communicating with me now, saying:

'_____,
(Your name)

you are my beloved!'

(See Romans 1:7).

You Are Love Poured Out

*L*ord, it is good to chat, and I find myself looking forward to meeting you. Let me start by telling you my best thinking about you. I know the beautiful statement of St John, that 'God is love' (*Jn.3:8-16*). But your love can't be thought of as static. It is always being poured out, inexhaustibly and richly. You yourself use the term 'poured out' at the Last Supper, I notice. Often the Holy Spirit is described as being 'poured out' on everyone.

Perhaps it is your very nature to be poured out, and this is at the heart of the universe? I have an image of this love as a great waterfall: am I being invited to come ever closer to it and to be drenched by its spray? Is this the deepest meaning of my life, whether I know it or not? Am I being constantly called into an unfathomable depth of loving relationships, since you, who are three divine persons, endlessly pour out your love on each other and on me too? Could it be that I, like a child, am being invited to 'dance' with you? Perhaps you are untiringly calling to me, 'we'd like you to make a fourth!'

Some writers speak about the endless laughter of the divine persons. One author says: 'In the core of the Trinity the Father laughs and gives birth to the Son. The Son laughs back at the Father and gives birth to the Spirit. The whole Trinity laughs and gives birth to you!' It does me good, Lord, to feel that I share in the laughter that rings across the universe. You yourself have said, 'blessed are you who weep, because you shall laugh'. Don't let me confuse divine intimacy with solemnity: you are a laughing as well as a loving God! You are indeed love that pours itself out.

$\mathcal{L}$ord, may I believe that you are communicating with me now, saying:

'

_____,
(Your name)

I have loved you with an everlasting love, and therefore I am constant in my affection for you.'

(See Jeremiah 31:3)

3

You Belong To Me

*D*ear God, the image of the divine that I live with is the image of Jesus. And that is what the Incarnation is all about: you make yourself accessible to me through your Son. He belongs to the human race: he's one of us, as we say! So when I want to know what you are like, I can go to the gospels and watch you in action in the person of Jesus. I learn how you relate to me by watching how Jesus relates to those he met. He is the face of the divine: the Father's face shines on him because he always keeps you in view. I might shine a bit better if I were to keep you in view in the same way.

C S Lewis says that when he wanted to get a few days off school, he would sit close to a boy who had just got over the measles. If he wanted to get wet, he had to stand in the rain. So, if he wanted to be like God, he had to get close to Jesus. By staying close to you I can become more like you in my loving. Growing in love is hard work, but it needs to happen in me. By staying near you something of you will rub off on me: that will be a good infection indeed! Help me always to want you, like the man who said, 'I must get to him (Jesus) because he belongs to me', or the woman who said, 'if I could only touch the hem of his garment.'

This knowing of you, Jesus, is meant to be a heart-to-heart affair: the more I know how totally your heart is set on me, the more I am drawn to love you in return. You have given yourself over to me; you belong to me and I to you. Help me to believe this.

*L*ord, may I believe that you are communicating with me now, saying:

'

_____
(Your name)

'

as the Father loves me, so I love you.
Please remain in my love!'

(See John 15:9)

4

Goodness Of A Deeper Kind

*L*ord, we speak of you as being 'the one from whom comes everything that is good'. That's a beautiful statement about you, and shows how easily I can be in touch with you. All I have to do is to notice any good thing – the view from my window, my computer, my hands as they type, **those I love,** the people I meet today – and connect them with you. This would turn a lot of my distractions into songs of gratitude. I need to become more contemplative, which means taking a long, loving look at the real world and discovering you behind it.

But, dear God, can I say that you are *simply* good? Be patient with me: you know better than I that the suffering and evil of the world turn so many people away from you, and you allow pain and tragedy rather than eliminating them. So while I rightly say you are good because of all the good that enfolds me, I must also say that your goodness is much more complex than that of a Santa Claus or a benevolent aunt or uncle. A lot of bad things happen in our world, so I have to ask how you convert them into good.

Can I say that while you are the source of all that is directly good, you also work hard on everything that is bad, in order to draw good out of it? You are set against suffering, evil and death, as your Son showed throughout his life: he cured all forms of sickness, he challenged evil and he raised people from the dead. In the Passion he was overwhelmed by suffering, evil and death, but he transformed them so that they became the occasion of great good. He turned everything inside out and so changed the history of the world, and so bad Friday became 'Good Friday'. Your goodness is of a deeper kind than mine: it embraces what is bad in order to turn it to good.

$\mathcal{L}$ord, may I believe that you are communicating with me now, saying:

'

_____
(Your name)
'

I love the world so much that I gave my only Son so that no-one may be lost but all may have eternal life.'

(See John 3:16)

5

Your Disfigured Images

*D*ear Lord, a desperate letter has just come to me from a Sister who runs a children's shelter in Bangkok. Though short of staff and funds, she takes in abandoned children. One, a three year old, was found rooting in a rubbish dump to survive. Her father was a violent drunkard and a drug addict. Her mother ran away with the little child and became a prostitute to survive, but suffered beatings from her 'customers' and tried to commit suicide. Many of the children in the shelter have been physically and sexually abused. HIV positive, they suffer from depression and are prone to self-harm.

Now, Lord, what have you to say to me that could help any of these children? They are your damaged and broken images. You never intended that their lives would turn out like this. Why don't you intervene to save them from these horrors? Help me on this!

Your thoughts and your ways, Lord, are not mine. I'm too small to see how you can allow so much pain and horror without intervening directly. But what I do see is a brave woman in Bangkok who may well have the questions I have, but is doing all she can to help these children. She is their only ray of hope. Yet, as of this moment I have come to know about her desperate need and her heroic efforts. Are you in fact intervening by calling out to me, 'Give her what you can!' Is it in ways like this that you undermine the evil of the world and also make me grow in love?

$\mathcal{L}$ord, may I believe that you are communicating with me now, saying:

'

_____,

(Your name)

you are the light of the world,
so let your light shine!'

(See Matthew 5:16)

6

God, Who Are You?

*D*ear God, because you are purest mystery you can't be grasped, and so I must simply let you be and let you speak. If I can be quiet inside and just let the words of your love notes fall into my heart like drops of water on a sponge, they will bear fruit. Is this how I can come to know you as you are?

What you were trying to get across to Moses when you said 'I am who I am'? Were you saying, 'I am simply myself; I need no explaining'? Is this what it means to be the creator – to be comfortably secure in your own existence? My existence, on the other hand, is not in my hands: it depends totally on you. I'm like a song: if you stop singing me, empty silence would follow. A great physicist surprised his students by saying that the world is made not of matter but of music: the world's continuing existence depends on you!

Years ago I dropped the image of you as the old bearded man in the clouds. Since you simply *are*, there can be no adequate image of you. You're more like a blue sky: blue symbolises heaven, serene and peaceable. A blue sky points to the divine: it is beautiful and unlimited, like you, and it encompasses everything.

Small children educate me best about you. For them, everything is a source of wonder – each person, each thing, each moment is unique and special. 'Children's faces, looking up; holding wonder like a cup.' Let me be like them, and so live even now in the kingdom of heaven.

$\mathcal{L}$ord, may I believe that you are communicating with me now, saying:

'
_____,
(Your name)

*I am never far from you,
for it is in me that you live and
move and have your being.*'

(See Acts 17:27)

7

You're The Great Giver

*L*ord, St Ignatius speaks of you as the lover who is always giving to the beloved – that's me! – and he adds that God wants to be given fully to me so far as can be. From personal experience St Ignatius believed that the only thing that holds back your gifts is my inability to notice and receive them. Help me, Lord, to notice the giftedness that is attached to everything and everyone around me. Life is all around me, so let me walk in it, admire it, take joy in it. But most of all let me see it all as your personal gift to me. I am a *gifted* person!

I don't want to think of you as someone far away who sends me gifts from a distance. I prefer to imagine that we gaze together on the same things, like a contented couple on a river bank who watch the water flow quietly by. So now I settle at the window with you and grow quiet, then I think of how you see what I see: blue sky, white clouds, trees and flowers, the red brick hospital, traffic on the road, people walking past. Teach me to see these ordinary things as you see them, that is, contemplatively – with a long loving look. You see all that is made, in its wholeness, and you see it as good. So I can hear or watch the daily news with you: it's news of the people that you love and care about. This softens things: traffic, for instance, is no longer simply traffic but your beloveds going by, and I find myself invited to wish them well, as you do. Bit by bit I see more through your eyes, and my gaze becomes loving and contemplative: I see things as your gift to me.

$\mathcal{L}$ord, may I believe that you are communicating with me now, saying:

'

———————————————————— ,

(Your name)

my right hand holds you fast,
and turns everything
to your good.'

(See Psalm 63:8; Romans 8:28)

8

Are You Fussy About My Failings?

ear God, when I sift through the Bible I find that many disturbing things are said about you: that you can be angry, jealous, destructive. It's quite confusing, if I am to be honest. But the heart of your message is that you love us infinitely, and you invite us to live out our lives in that certainty. This raises the issue of sin. How about my wrong doing? I can feel embarrassed that I can't recall when I was last at Confession, but can I dare to ask if you are less preoccupied about my wrong doing than I used to think? Given your infinite love, perhaps you really don't delay on my failings but instead immediately look to see how you can get me going again on the road of love?

The best image Jesus gives of you is that of the prodigal father: he doesn't wait until his son crawls up on his knees, instead he starts running to him, which a Jewish father should never do! He doesn't listen to his son's confession, instead he throws his arms around him—what will the servants think?! – restores him to his status as son with the ring, the robe, the sandals and then calls for a great feast.

Perhaps the worst thing I can do when I spoil our relationship or hurt someone is to try to hide from you, as Adam did. 'I was afraid, so I hid'. Let me instead turn to you and say, 'Now look what I've done!' May I find a compassionate smile which says, 'yes, but now let us move on together'. In response I say 'will you help me find ways to repair the damage caused by my failings?'

There's a poem titled, 'Shut up, I'm going to sing you a Love Song' and that's just what the father does. I like it! Thanks for singing it to me.

$\mathcal{L}$ord, may I believe that you are communicating with me now, saying:

'
_____,
(Your name)

*I blot out your wrongdoings,
and I will not remember your sins.*'

(See Isaiah 43:25)

9

Quality Time With You

*A*n older Jesuit friend once said to me, 'I don't know any more what's going on between me and God: either I'm praying all the time or I'm not praying at all!'

Lord, that honesty is helpful to me as I age. My prayer used to be more structured; I'd try to become still, ask for the grace I wanted, read the gospel of the day, imagine myself in the scene, ask Jesus what he was trying to teach me. After thirty minutes I'd wrap my prayer package up neatly with an Our Father and go off contented to breakfast!

Now my prayer is a bit of a shambles: dull, unfocused, distracted. Sometimes I don't pray: instead I do 'something useful' like helping someone, or even writing pages like this! Yet, I'm aware that I'm missing something when I don't give even a little daily quality time to you. It may seem as if it's an empty waiting, as when I'm flicking through the magazines in the surgery when the doctor is delayed. It's empty time, perhaps, but it's not wasted! Just to sit for a bit, with my icon and my lighted candle, shows that I want you more than anything else. Perhaps my distracted mind and empty heart are the best symbols of generosity that I can muster up. You work well in barrenness, as Scripture shows: so where there are no obstructions perhaps your grace can work in me at depths I know little of.

Perhaps too my life mirrors my prayer – no great order in it: bits and bobs, kindnesses, interruptions, glad surprises. But like a tired pilgrim, so long as I am walking the road that is leading to my goal, which is you, perhaps all my plodding time is not wasted but quality time.

$\mathcal{L}$ord, may I believe that you are communicating with me now, saying:

'

_____,

(Your name)

the Spirit comes to help you in your weakness. For when you cannot pray properly the Spirit expresses your plea in a way that could never be put into words.'

(See Romans 8:26)

Darkness And Disaster

*L*ord, awareness of your love can slip away from my heart so easily, whenever there's a disaster I begin to doubt it. My small mind starts whirling, and I ask, 'How could you do this to me?' or 'How could you let that happen to someone else?' The dark side of things can so quickly eclipse the light. I say – excuse me for this! – 'Where the hell are you gone?' My demons then have a field day.

Let me instead watch out for your way of going about things. At the beginning, you tell us, darkness lay over the face of the earth then, first of all your works, you created light. Why did you let darkness have its place; why not obliterate it? But light and darkness *both* have their place in your scheme of things. This helps me! It makes me less surprised at the darkness that is around and focuses me on the fact that the light will come back. I should not expect a world without some darkness.

Because you come into the world as divine light, darkness is pushed back and can't eclipse it. I should focus on you as light, holding the darkness at bay, dealing resourcefully with suffering and evil. In another world perpetual light will shine on us all, but for now help me to live in the light myself and to battle the darkness as you do. After all I am infinitely loved and you need me to be 'the light of the world'. May I believe that patient endurance illuminates what is dark from the inside. So it was on Calvary and can be in my life too.

*L*ord, may I believe that you are
communicating with me now, saying:

'

_____,
(Your name)

if you should walk through the valley of
darkness, you need fear no evil.
I am there with my rod and my
staff to give you comfort.'

(See Psalm 23:4)

You Are For Me

*L*ord, you want our world to be a safe and friendly place in which we can grow to our fullness. Although we mess up both ourselves and our fragile world, you're always at work for our good. You restore and re-create what we spoil: that must keep you busy! What is to come will reveal the fullness of your loving: it won't be a sorting out of the bad from the good – it doesn't take God to do that—but, against all the odds, the winning over of the bad. 'When *everything* is said and done, we are infinitely loved.' Such a brave statement in face of violence, hatred, wars, murders and betrayals of every sort – all the bad stuff of our daily news. This teaches me to be patient with myself, with others, and with all institutions, including the Church.

Dear God, from your point of view, ultimately I have nothing to be afraid of. The light at the end of the tunnel is the light of God. And you are *for* me, on my side. I love that small word, 'for': it sums up Christian faith. '*For* us, and *for* our salvation'. 'He was crucified *for* us.' In symbol and in word you show that you are *for* us at the Last Supper: 'This is my body, given up *for* you: this is the cup of my blood, poured out *for* you.' You are God who is infinitely *for* us.

In turn, I am to be *for* my sisters and brothers. You intend one single community of love, in which everyone, divine and human, is *for* everyone else. The growth of that community depends in part on me. May those around me find that I am unreservedly *for* them, just as you are. Then I will be in harmony with you.

$\mathcal{L}$ord, may I believe that you are communicating with me now, saying:

'

_____ ,

do not be afraid, for I have redeemed you.
I have called you by your name:
you are mine.'

(See Isaiah 43:1)

12

Your View Of Success

*D*ear Jesus, what is success? We all want it for ourselves and for those we love. But for many people life is a ghastly failure: they don't achieve their potential. I think of children who never get a chance and end up as part of the wreckage of life: no money, no job, no prospects, no stable and satisfying relationships. But as God surely you don't do failures? Have you a criterion for success which is deeper than ours? Show me!

Dear Jesus, was *your* life a success? By human standards you were a dreadful failure – after brief success you ended up being betrayed and denounced as a criminal, a liar and a fraud. Then after the most horrible of torments; you died and were buried. End of story. As the disciples on the Emmaus Road said, 'we had hoped, but it all fell apart…' But further along that same road, you come out with the extraordinary statement: 'Was it not appropriate that I should suffer and so enter into my glory?' Are you saying that your Father raised you from death because of the loving way you endured your passion? Deep in your soul did you know even at the worst of moments that you were infinitely loved?

Patient and loving endurance was all you had to show at the end. You made no money, carved out no empire, left no family. Success in divine eyes, then, must lie on another level. Messy and tragic though your life was, you managed to reveal through it a fullness of love which catches up the whole world and brings it safely home. In this way you verify our theme – that when everything is said and done, we *are* infinitely loved. So can I not say that real success in life is achieved simply by living lovingly?

$\mathcal{L}$ord, may I believe that you are communicating with me now, saying:

'

_____ ,

(Your name)

do not let your heart be troubled;
trust in God and trust in me.'

(See John 14:1)

13

Our Eternal Friendship

*D*ear God, do you really my desire friendship? I know something about human friendships, from family life, from groups of which I have been a member, and from the friends I have made. Friends make life bearable and joyful. Are these perhaps models of divine friendship? Is is it your great plan, to bring everyone into eternal friendship with yourself and with each other?

When you say you love me infinitely, are you saying that from your side, you and I are already friends and will always be? This means I am not alone, that we are in close partnership, and that is a great comfort. My well being is your central concern, and you are strong and resourceful. You move into action when things going wrong for me: I'm the half-dead traveller and you the good Samaritan. You carry me, heal me, pay my costs because I've lost everything. I can endure what life throws at me because you're at my side, 'a mighty hero', working away quietly for me. Your friendship is limitless: it stretches beyond death into sharing eternal joy.

Good friends share everything, and you share so much with me – all of creation is there for my good. From your Son I learn just how deeply you love me – so much that you laid down your life for me! There's no greater friendship than that. Friends share what they can, and you share everything with me, your wayward friend!

What can I give you in return? Make me grow in goodness and help me treasure our relationship, now and forever. Let me too share all your concerns for my needy brothers and sisters: they also are your friends.

$\mathcal{L}$ord, may I believe that you are communicating with me now, saying:

'

_____

(Your name)
'

as the Father loves me, so I love you.
You are my friend: abide in my love.'

(See John 15:7-15)

14

How Do You Manage The Mess?

*D*ear God, may I call you 'Lord of the Mess'? I'm writing this reflection as a London tower block is being gutted by fire. Hundreds endured smoke and fumes many were burnt beyond recognition. Such a mess. Each was your image and likeness. How could you allow them to die so terribly? Where were you? Where was your love?

In the life of your Son you show how you respond to the suffering of the world. Love alone would be your way, and that I understand because you are simply love that pours itself out. You have no other weapons. So you sent your beloved Son among us. He endured as we do the pain of human life, but it cost him not less than everything. He endures the depth of human malice, but his love transforms it into joy.

In the gospel story you reveal a breadth of love so wide that it encompasses sin and evil, suffering and death. Limits are set to them, but not to your love. I imagine Jesus' life, death and resurrection as the outer edges of a great jigsaw of which the pieces are the jumbled history of the world. Of course I can't yet see how most pieces can be fitted in: many of them are twisted and distorted, like the tower block. But the outline is clear: because you love us limitlessly you enter into our pain and death and defeat them at a radical level. The tragedies of evil and suffering are transformed into a new epic story, and in your good time we will be shown how you managed to make a masterpiece even out of the mess we can make of our beautiful world.

*L*ord, may I believe that you are communicating with me now, saying:

'

_____

(Your name)

I love you and gave myself up for you.'

(See Galatians 2:20)

15

Mission Impossible?

*L*ord, do you delight in working against seemingly impossible odds? Your ways of thinking are so different from mine, and that's good, because my thinking is so small and unimaginative. I get overwhelmed and discouraged so easily when things go wrong, but not you. I am told it takes a smart person seven years to understand electrons, so how many years does it take to understand you, the creator of electrons, protons, neutrons, quarks and gluons – the lot? But while you manage the physical world very well, can you manage us humans when we spoil things? When the sad history of humankind is all said and done will you still achieve your dream? Or is yours an impossible dream?

I speak of the mystery of evil, but to you it's not a mystery at all. Keep reminding me that in your Son you overcame evil and pain, not on the surface level but at their source; you prefer to work from the inside out. You labour endlessly and sensitively to soften our hearts so that we turn toward goodness rather than evil. Even I have noticed a delicate mellowing in my own heart over the years, and I often see this in others too. It's slow work, however, but you're giving yourself plenty of time! 13.8 billion years have gone into the present situation, and perhaps you will allow billions more before the human drama concludes by your love winning out in everything.

You advise me in the Bible that while many things are impossible to me, *nothing* is impossible to you. You are saying, 'Trust me on this: I can manage.' Your promise can act as a beam of light by which I can safely pick my steps along the valley of darkness.

$\mathcal{L}$ord, may I believe that you are
communicating with me now, saying:

'
_____ ,

(Your name)

in the wilderness I carried you,
just as a parent carries their child,
all the way that you travelled until
you reached this place.'

(See Deuteronomy 1:31)

16

Do I Really Matter To You?

*D*ear Lord, recently I read of someone who felt that other people's profiles were drawn in strong black, or in colour with magic markers, but hers was sketched only in light pencil. I sometimes feel like that woman, almost invisible, unimportant. Maybe it goes with seniority!

Psychologists tell us that to be truly alive someone else's loving gaze is needed: otherwise we can never blossom to our full potential. I know you do your best to provide everyone with good parents, they're a great blessing to a child, but of course this doesn't always happen. You also send us good grandparents, relatives, friends who help us to believe we are worthwhile. They are escorts of your loving care. You want us to receive your great gift, the conviction that we are OK, that we are loved and that we matter.

May your word today convince me that I am good, worthwhile, lovable and wonderful; that I am your beloved, your unique creation, the apple of your eye. May I believe that, no matter what, you love me infinitely, that you embrace me tenderly and live within me and that you have dreams for me that go way beyond my own. For you, I will always be important! My core identity is that I am your beloved! You are, so to speak, part of my DNA.

If I could see myself as I am in your eyes everything would slip into place. Not only am I important to you but I am important for the world. What I am by your gift helps to draw the whole world nearer to God. Let me live out of this rich mystery and be happy about myself, and my low profile. You yourself seem to like a low profile too.

$\mathcal{L}$ord, may I believe that you are communicating with me now, saying:

'

—————————————————————————,

(Your name)

I have made you little less than the angels, and crowned you with glory and honour. Your name is inscribed on the palms of my hands.'

(See Psalm 8:5; Isaiah 49:16)

17

Can I Trust Your Plan?

*L*ord, I spend my days making little plans: how to get from here to there, what to write about, what to spend my time at, how to look after my health…

So I'm a planner. Sometimes my plans work out, other times not. Recently I was driving a friend to the airport. We stopped for a message but the car wouldn't start again. Time was short: what to do? I was pretty wound up, as you remember, Lord, and said a little prayer – 'Get me out of this!' Next moment along came someone I knew. He happened – or so he kindly said – to be passing the airport, so my friend hopped in and got her flight. I was stranded till the AA came, but that didn't matter too much.

Now, Lord, that doesn't happen for you: your plans are comprehensive, they take account of everything, including the freedom you have given me as a human being. You don't get surprised by things that go wrong. Your plans have an elastic quality: they stretch as needed. You support my well intentioned plans so that they bear fruit disproportionate to my little efforts. Other times you save me when my bright ideas are heading for disaster. My plans are always provisional, they depend on factors outside my control, but yours won't fail. Your plans are wise and loving, crafted for the good of the whole human race, no matter how chaotic the world may seem. Things may be against me, or against someone I love but your plans are *for* me, and your resources are unlimited. I often go astray, but your plans cover all contingencies, so I can't get totally lost. I can trust your plans.

$\mathcal{L}$ord, may I believe that you are communicating with me now, saying:

'

_____ ,
(Your name)

I know the plans I have in mind for you,
plans for peace and not disaster,
to give you a future full of hope.'

(See Jeremiah 29:11)

18

The One Thing That Matters

*L*ord, I've been reflecting about your plan and I was reminded of the story of Martha and Mary. In Bethany you saw that Martha was so worked up about getting your dinner that she was angry with her sister who was doing nothing to help; she was just sitting with you and absorbing every word you said. You intervened and asked Martha not to fuss, not to lose sight of the one thing that really matters. You were afraid that Martha's anxiety to do a good job would eclipse her love, that love which alone would make her work fruitful. In her anxiety to offer you a good meal she wasn't looking after her own needs; she was out of tune with what you called the essential.

What had Martha to learn? You weren't saying that getting meals ready for others is not important. Rather you were offering a context for Martha's labours. 'Seek first the kingdom of God' was your slogan. Now 'the kingdom of God' really means 'God' and God means 'love'. We are then to try to be loving in all we do. You yourself, Lord, do everything out of love, and you're saying that love is that precious quality that gives a divine and lasting quality to our work. Without love, it seems, we are trading with worthless currency. A busy woman – like Martha – once expressed the essential by saying 'I must do things in love and freedom or leave them alone'. In a l'Arche community members were asked not to do the cooking if they couldn't do it lovingly! Help me to do everything in love, and so make all my tasks a prayer.

$\mathcal{L}$ord, may I believe that you are communicating with me now, saying:

'

_____

(Your name)
'

I am standing at your door, knocking. If you open the door, I will come in and share a meal with you'.

(See Revelation 3:20)

A Heart As Wide As Yours

*L*ord, as these precious love notes, from Scripture, begin to take root in me, I notice that I am becoming a little less self-concerned. Your incalculable love of me means that I don't have to defend my small store of love against the demands of other people. You abundantly meet my need for love, and so I can share the love in my heart instead of hoarding it. It is for sharing. I am becoming what human beings are meant to be, sharers of love. Just as you love me for myself and not for how I respond, I want to love others with the same non-demanding love. Their poor response puts me off less now: my love is becoming purer. Others are to be loved as fragile fellow creatures held in your love. My heart is not yet as wide as yours, but I want it to be so.

There seem to be two steps in your intentions for me: first, that I become aware that I am passionately loved by you and second, that I let go of my little self and put others first. You are the one who is secure in your love and so you put others first, and I'm edging that way, even if it's like a dance where I take two steps forward and one backward. I no longer need so much to have myself at the centre of my world: instead your love of me is happily engaging my surprised attention more and more. I find I can accept people more for themselves: I can even find happiness in giving myself away – which is what parents and grandparents and all good folk do. It's also what you do. The Eucharist is a recurring reminder of that I am to be like the bread; bread blessed, broken, given, consumed. I'm getting the message!

$\mathcal{L}$ord, may I believe that you are communicating with me now, saying:

'

_____

(Your name)

my steadfast love for you is from everlasting to everlasting.'

(See Psalm 103:17)

20

My Friend Stefan

*L*ord, on this lovely morning I went on a stroll along the canal, where I met Stefan. He is from Budapest, speaks little English and came to Ireland hoping for a job. He now has a spot on the canal bank: he is dropped off by his 'manager' and there he begs. He's in middle years, tanned and gaunt, but still has a sparkle in his eyes. How long will he last? The man before him died a few months ago, and another drowned, 'unwept, unhonoured and unsung'.

Now if I were you, I would save Stefan from his plight. You respect the rhythms of human living, however, and instead of stepping in and preventing suffering, you engage with it at depth. You take up the cross of the world and invite me to share with you in this task. No armchair salvation will do. I'm meant to be a Simon of Cyrene in my time and place. And you work on my heart through poor Stefan, to break it open so that my love – the love you lavish on me – may flow to him. Stefan and I can help one another. In him I find you suffering, and in my tiny way I can help to relieve at least a bit of his pain. You want us to liberate people from their pain as you did yourself; you want me to help to take others down from their crosses. If I can offer a moment's relief to one of your 'little ones' like Stefan, let me do it. I can give him a few euro towards a meal, show him my respect, engage with him and make him feel that he is still linked in to the rest of human kind by a simple bond of love.

$\mathcal{L}$ord, may I believe that you are communicating with me now, saying:

'_____,'

(Your name)

do not despise one of these little ones,
because their angels continually
see my Father's face.'

(See Matthew 18:10)

21

My Love Story

*D*ear God, is each of us a book telling the story of your love? Is mine a love story too, in all its ups and downs, its shadows and its light-filled times? To me my story is pretty ordinary, hardly a best seller! My image of myself is of someone who has plodded along quietly; nothing very dramatic seems to have happened. No publisher would want my manuscript – it wouldn't sell.

But if I catch on to the fact that my unremarkable story is co-authored, everything suddenly changes. If you are steadily working on me deep down, to make me grow in love and so become like you, then I can look back on the chapters of my life with new interest, to see what you – my unobtrusive ghost-writer – have been up to over many years. What I thought of as simply 'my story' is in fact better called 'our story': you and I write it together. Our storyline is rich, the makings of an epic, worthy of a special edition with gold lettering.

And I get amazed that everyone else's story is also being co-authored. The theme is the same, though intensely intimate to each. And because you're involved I can never write off an awkward person with the remark, 'Well, Lord, you're not getting too far with her!' I heard of a man whose neighbour had died he said, 'sure, he died years ago but they forgot to bury him'. I need to see people differently: each of us has our own secret scripture, and you tell no-one any story but their own. Life gets exciting when I view people like this and try to spot your hand on their messy pages. Is each of us a vital chapter in the love story of the cosmos? Wow!

$\mathcal{L}$ord, may I believe that you are
communicating with me now, saying:

'

_____'
(Your name)

*When Christ who is your life is revealed,
then you also will be
revealed with him in glory.'*

(See Colossians 3:4)

22

No Boundaries To Loving

*L*ord, when I look back I feel that from infancy onward, there was never a time in my life when there wasn't a difficult person to cope with. I don't want to suggest that you set me up for this, but I do say that the stretching of my little heart has gone on endlessly, sometimes almost to breaking point. I am forced to accept others as they are, not as I would prefer them to be.

You work in all my encounters, undermining my defences and challenging me to become a person whose heart is without barriers, limits and boundaries. You want me to be accepting and inclusive because that's how you are yourself. I must not exclude anyone from my love, so I find myself praying for all those whom, in an earlier phase of my life, I would have turned my back on. You shine on good and bad alike, and I must at least wish well to everyone, since that is the most basic level of loving.

My own weaknesses should make me more tolerant of the weaknesses and foibles of others. My diminishments – declining health and energy, loss of friends, becoming more peripheral to affairs where I used have a more central role – these can make my heart more spacious. I am being hollowed out, bit by bit, in order that I may love more.

In my death I will be a totally empty space, but it will be filled by you. I can then look beyond death to becoming radiant with your love, and the details of my life will then be seen to have been your infinitely wise and rich preparation.

$\mathcal{L}$ord, may I believe that you are communicating with me now, saying:

'_____,'

(Your name)

I am all compassion and love.'

(See Psalm 102:8)

23

The Amen Of My Life

*L*ord, it is you who will write the final chapter of my life, with little help from me. Yet, I have a contribution to make! Let me accept my life as it will be at its close, and offer it to you now, because I may be incapable of doing it at the time of my death. Please read my tale with a kindly eye! Forgive the flawed beauty of your work of art.

Let me then take a blank sheet, and on the top left write, 'Dear God' and at the bottom right put my name, and underneath it 'Amen'. That's the framework of all my days. I can fill the space in the middle – in my imagination at least – with my activities and accomplishments, my sufferings and my failures. In saying 'Amen' I will have the last word!

I hand everything to you and ask you to bring good out of it. My 'Amen' says, 'Lord, this is the song of my life. It's flat in places, it's a mix of grace and failure, and I've bungled the words and the melody here and there, but it's me. I love you and dedicate my song to you. My days and years are like the water pots at Cana: they need your creating touch to be turned into good wine. Let me believe that even when everything about me is said and done, I am infinitely loved! In my every choice you are edging me to the more loving option. In things that go wrong for me, illnesses, accidents or the deaths of those I love, you are trying to help me to accept everything patiently and lovingly. And since only love will remain at the end, let me from now on fill my days with love.

*L*ord, may I believe that you are communicating with me now, saying:

'

_____,

(Your name)

my Father and I will love you,
and we will come to you and
make our home with you.'

(See John 14:23)

God, Why Hide Yourelf?

God, you are good at disguising yourself, and you must enjoy doing that! The older I get, the more mysterious you become. Everything is pregnant with the divine – everything is, as it were, a caress of God, but in a hidden way. I am walking around in *your* great world: it is not mine. You invite me to proceed with a sense of wonder and awe: the lights are amber, not red or green! You are educating me gently and sensitively. I am not yet ready for a face-to-face encounter with you, but you will decide when the time is right and then I shall see you unveiled, and indeed become like you.

But for now, let me look at some of your disguises so that I may learn 'to greet you the days I meet you, and bless when I understand'. I need these 'Aha!' moments to keep me going in the right direction.

You came to Abraham in the disguise of three strangers but Abraham and Sarah caught on and gave you hospitality, and you blessed the world through them. You came in disguise to Elijah in his cave: you weren't in the storm, the earthquake or the fire but in the whisper of the wind, and he knew it was you. The Israelites at Sinai knew you through dramatic signs: cloud, earthquake, thunder and a mighty voice. The Prophets recognised you speaking in the depths of their hearts.

Mary recognised you in an angel's request: shepherds and wise men caught on to your disguise as a helpless baby. Your teaching and miracles helped the open minded to recognise you under the disguise of a carpenter's son. But, dear Lord, as we shall see, at the end of your life you used even more puzzling disguises. Truly you are a hidden God.

*L*ord, may I believe that you are communicating with me now, saying:

'

_____,
(Your name)

my thoughts are not your thoughts, nor are your ways my ways. As the heavens are higher than the earth, so are my ways higher than your ways.'

(See Isaiah 55:8-9).

'Aha!' Moments

*J*esus, help me to continue to track your disguises so that I may be alert to the endless ways you are present to me. I don't want to miss you as you pass by.

You stripped yourself of divine glory in becoming just like us, so it took a leap of faith for people to identify you and say, 'Look, there goes God!' But then came your passion: surely God can't be tortured and killed! Your disguise was then complete. Your enemies said, 'come down from that cross, then we'll believe your claims'. You didn't. You kept your disguise. If you were God, then it seemed that God is dead.

But then you rose from the dead, only to disguise yourself again – as the gardener, the traveller on Emmaus Road, the visitor who asked for something to eat and the man standing on the lake shore at dawn. You gave hints: your message of peace, your forgiveness, your special way of breaking bread, your wounds – these helped doubting disciples, each in their own time, to reach their 'Aha!' moment. Was this slow revelation a kindness for us who cannot bear too much reality?

Can I bear the shock of bumping into you? Is this why you still like to conceal yourself? You identify now with my needy neighbours – a massive range of disguises! But however well camouflaged, each is your image and likeness, a brother or sister for whom you died. You are in people wherever they gather in goodwill. And what about bread, wine, water, oil and sacred words? They're symbols of your presence! Lord, it's almost too much, but let me experience more and more the glad surprise of bumping into you everywhere, and saying 'Aha!'

$\mathcal{L}$ord, may I believe that you are communicating with me now, saying:

'

_____
(Your name)
,

Whatever you did to the least of my sisters and brothers, you did it to me!

(See Matthew 25:40).

26

Escort Of Your Love

*P*atrick arrives in an AIDS hospice in Paris weak and emaciated, with lesions all over his legs. Still handsome at twenty-four, he loves beauty: he worked at making jewellery. Always solitary, he had left home because he could not bear to tell his parents he was gay. Now he can't tell them he has AIDS. Surrounded now by a dedicated nursing team he allows himself to be tended to. The love and support of the staff amaze him, given that his flesh is rotting and gives off a sickening odour. He sees that it's not just his body the staff are looking after, but his person. No longer cut off from human contact, he improves, and even contacts his family. Although he knows he will soon die, he goes back to his apartment for a short respite and designs jewellery again: this time two candlesticks, named Hope and Love.

Back in the hospice he is beginning to see the world with new eyes. His original self-focused concern is shifting to the goodness of the nurses. He observes them all his waking hours. 'I couldn't do what they do' he says 'but I try to put myself in their place.' He smiles and this transforms things. He grieves for his mother in her anguish. On his final night the nurse thanks him for all he has given to the staff through his endurance, asks him not to be anxious but to allow himself to be taken home.

Lord, this helps me see how you want to work through me to help people to realise they are loved. I am to be an escort of your infinite love wherever someone is in need.

$\mathcal{L}$ord, may I believe that you are communicating with me now, saying:

'

(Your name)

I love a cheerful giver, and I am able to provide you with blessings in abundance'.

(See 2 Corinthians 9:7-8)

27

'Please Be Seated!'

esus, you liked to take your meals with sinners and outcasts. This makes me wonder about the seating arrangements at that great wedding feast which we call heaven. When I arrive will you come along with a big welcoming smile and say, 'Now, where would you like to sit?' I'd look and see on one side of the enormous hall a huge gathering of people, many of them quite disreputable types, others poor and unwashed. But there's a terrific buzz at their tables: they are delighted that you treat them as your honoured guests. There's the prodigal son telling stories of his time away from home, and the Samaritan woman explaining what life had been like with five husbands. I'd be wondering how I'd fit in with this merry lot as they get down to sampling the varied delights of your great banquet.

Then I look at the other side: tables for one or at most two, serious types there; no fun, no joy. They glare at the boisterous group and mutter in cold rage, 'That crowd has no right to be here, they should be in hell. But we have our rights!' Then I hear your voice, 'I'm still wondering where you'd prefer to sit. Perhaps you need a little more time, so if you like, why not stand aside while I seat the people behind you?' I say, 'I want to sit where you sit.'

Lord, enlarge my heart so that I may come to accept everyone and condemn none of your invited guests. Only then will I be able to sit at ease with you.

*L*ord, may I believe that you are communicating with me now, saying:

'_____'

(Your name)

I have prepared a banquet for you. You will have the fullness of joy in my presence, and at my right hand happiness forever.'

(See Psalm 23: 5-6)

28

You Are The God Who Cares

Lord, someone I know broke a leg in a motorbike accident and landed in A&E. Lonely and afraid, he rang his best friend and left a message. A text came back: 'Sorry: hate hospitals. Call when you get out.' It was the end of their relationship, as the biker said, 'If someone doesn't really care when you're in trouble, they're nothing to you'.

Lord, often I go about my affairs and endure my troubles as if you aren't interested, as if you'd made the world and then stood back, leaving me to get on with my life. But that's not fair to you! Instead of turning to you only when I'm at crisis point, make me realise that you care for me in every detail of my life. That's what your love is about. You're always watching out for me, planning what is best for me and setting things up in ways that will help me.

You have a dream for me. And you work to make it come true. You're always knocking at my door, waiting to be invited in. You love to chat with me about all that's going on for me. Even brief moments with you give me confidence that we can manage anything that comes up. You never say, 'Not available. Give me a call later.' Even if I'm upset and don't think to call you, you are already working to undo any mess I may have landed in. Your care is limitless – it reaches into eternity, so meeting up with you is always creative and healing for me. As true friends we can chat about everything, good, bad and problematic. You have something wise to offer about every situation, so let me keep in close touch with you always.

$\mathcal{L}$ord, may I believe that you are communicating with me now, saying:

'

————————————————————,

(Your name)

when you were a child I loved you.
It was I who taught you to walk.
I led you with cords of human kindness:
I was like those who lift infants to their cheeks.
I bent down to you and fed you.'

(See Hosea 11:1-4)

29

In The Remedial Class

ord, so many people die suddenly, with no time to amend their ways. So how do you make them grow in love such that they can feel fully at home in eternal life with you? And whatever about them, what about me?

Will my encounter with you in death have a searing quality in which all falsehoods melt away, such that I become free at last to choose you with my whole heart and soul? Was this Peter's experience in his unexpected encounter with you on the shore of Lake Galilee? You took him aside, addressed him by name and asked him three times: 'Do you love me?' Surely his betrayals of you flashed through his heart, painfully burning away all self-defence, but leaving him healed and able to say, 'Lord, you know everything; you know I love you.' His meeting with you, as his crucified and risen Lord, must have had a painful dimension, yet it was your infinite love at work, *a searing light*, liberating and life giving.

If I call this 'purgatory' then what will happen in death will be a *remedial education in loving*. It's remedial education because love should have been the touchstone for all that I did or endured, but it wasn't. So our encounter will involve the melting of my stubborn heart, till I no longer hold out against you or indeed against anyone in this world. Your forgiveness, flooding through me, will make me want to seek forgiveness of all those I have injured in any way. Perhaps I'll find people coming to ask my forgiveness too? And since, when everything is said and done, we are all infinitely loved, will we all join hands in friendship and dance together with you, forever?

$\mathcal{L}$ord, may I believe that you are communicating with me now, saying:

'

_____ ,

(Your name)

do you love me?'

(See John 21:17)

30

You Will Be My Joy

Lord, when for the last time my eyes close on this world, what will happen to me? Will I sink into empty darkness as I return to the dust from which I came? Is there any hope of rescue from this oblivion?

I rely on your repeated promise of eternal life: the term recurs some seventeen times in St John's Gospel alone. Help me to believe that I will awaken from death to your kindly presence, and that you will take me by the hand and lead me into abundant life. Then I will see that this life, with all its trials, was a preparation for something infinitely better. As patients dream of what they will do when discharged from hospital, students make plans for life after graduation, let me dream of what life will be like when I come to enjoy the freedom of the children of God?

Surely I will be happy beyond all my hopes and dreams, and that happiness will centre on the full flowering of my relationship with you. You will take me home to yourself, so that we may be together for evermore. You will be my lasting joy. I will be caught into the happiness that you, Father, Son and Spirit, enjoy with one another. I will sense myself being loved in an overwhelming way. Surely my small heart will burst open with gratitude in fully becoming your adopted child, called by name, welcomed and embraced, my friends beside me, my inheritance awaiting me. Lord, you are just so good: thank you!

$\mathcal{L}$ord, may I believe that you are communicating with me now, saying:

'

_____ ,

(Your name)

no eye has seen and no ear has heard,
nor can you even imagine all that
I have prepared for you!'

(See 1 Corinthians 2:9)

31

Free To Love Like You

Dear Lord, I like the Chinese proverb which says that if you want to be happy for a lifetime, help others. Now I know from experience that that is true for this life, but when we all find ourselves at home with you I presume there will be no-one in need of help. I will, however, become free endlessly to love others just as they are. That is the dynamic of your life as Trinity, and it will be mine when I become like you. Here my happiest relationships are tinged with the awareness that they will end with death, but in your home all will be secure: no more frustrations, heartbreaks, estrangements, jealousy or sadness. Instead the beauty, goodness, freedom and joy which are yours, Lord, will radiate through each of us. There will be one undivided love, and all I have lost will be restored to me. Joy will be the serious business of heaven.

All things grow with love, so my less-than-attractive flaws will fade away. I will no longer need to be defensive, aggressive, shy, dominant or whatever. When accepted as I am, my hidden goodness and potential will begin to flower. I will become fully myself, as will everyone around me. My creativity will be unbounded, so surely I will continue to play a unique if humble role in the unfolding of our world's sacred history?

Your providence will fascinate me endlessly: how you manage to make a glorious symphony out of the often discordant notes we provide you with, how you coax good out of the worst of situations and how you wrestle with sin, evil and death to make meaning grow out of even the most senseless things.

Let me then be patient and trusting, Lord, and accept present reality as it comes to me. When everything is said and done your infinite love will bring me safely home, and with me, all my sisters and brothers, and the cosmos itself. Amen.

$\mathcal{L}$ord, may I believe that you are communicating with me now, saying:

'

_____ '

(Your name)

*my power, working in you,
can do infinitely more than
you can ask or imagine.'*

(See Ephesians 3:20)

Some books by Brian Grogan SJ which expand on the hints given in the preceding pages.

To Grow in Love: A Spirituality of Ageing, Dying and Glory.
Dublin: Messenger Publications, 2017.

God, You're Breaking My Heart.
Dublin: Messenger Publications, 2016

Finding God in All Things.
Dublin: Messenger Publications, 2014.

Where To From Here? The Christian Vision of Life After Death.
Dublin: Veritas, 2011.

Our Graced Life Stories.
Dublin: Messenger Publications, 2000

Available at: www.messenger.ie